THE
ART OF SELLING
TOYS

THE ART OF SELLING TOYS

HARMAN CHHABRA

Worldwide Published by
Pendown Press

PENDOWN PRESS LLP
An ISO 9001 & ISO 14001 Certified Co.
Regd. Office 3767A, Kanhaiya Nagar,
Tri Nagar, Delhi-110035
Ph.: 8180886000, 9650072927, 8595249536
E-mail: info@pendownpress.com
Branch Office 1A/2A, 20, Hari Sadan, Ansari Road,
Daryaganj, New Delhi-110002
Ph.: 011-45794768
Website: PendownPress.com

First Edition: 2023

ISBN: 978-93-5554-647-0

"The story of toys in India has been very interesting since the time of independence, and more so after the entire game changed post the pandemic, where games such as board games & puzzles, DIY kits and Legos etc., that had taken a backseat to tabs & playstations made a comeback. The Indian Toy Story of the Millenials including the existential threat due to deep discounts etc. has been captured very well by the author."

~Maya Toys,
No.11 Aurobindo place market New Delhi-16

Contents

ABOUT THE AUTHOR

Hello, I am Harman Chhabra. I am a retail marketing strategist and the inventor and creator of the first-ever educational baby walker in India. I am committed to delivering the finest products and sharing all my learnings through this book, aiming to benefit toy retailers in India.

My journey in the toy industry began after completing my schooling. I pursued a specialized course in toy-making molds at a renowned university in Canada. After graduating, I joined my father's toy business, where I was fascinated to discover a wide range of toys.

But here's the hard truth:

When I entered the market and met the retailers, I was shocked to learn their side of the story. They were plagued with common problems such as low profits, low cash flow, fewer customers, credit problems, debt, and more. Despite my efforts to offer them the best products, they were resistant to trying anything new and stuck with the belief of "let what's selling, continue to sell."

I, too, became trapped in the same system and carried on for the next ten years with old-fashioned beliefs about business. However, something happened in the year 2017 that changed everything. I met a renowned retailer with a large toy store who was forced to shut down his shop due to intense competition in the market. It was the same retailer I had met when I first entered the business, and he was full of joy at that time.

This finding shocked me, and we discussed the reasons behind this situation. We concluded that only 4% of toy shops were utilizing different strategies that the remaining 96% were unaware of, resulting in them controlling 80% of the toy business.

That moment is one I will never forget. After seven years of arduous struggle, I finally unlocked the secret code of strategies used by successful toy shops to dominate the toy business. Now, my mission is to unleash the true potential of 10,000 toy retail shops in India by deciphering these strategies and sharing them in this book.

Today, the upliftment of toy shop retailers is an integral part of my life, and I embrace it with every breath I take.

I have been fortunate to work with many prominent retailers and toy manufacturers across the globe, including India's biggest retailer, FirstCry. I have learned a great deal from them.

While working in this industry, I have observed that most Indian toy shop owners start their business in a conventional way, and it's understandable when you are working your way up the ladder. However, as time passes, the business starts to grow, bringing along a host of associated problems.

Case Study of a Retailer Going from Zero to Hero

In this case study, we will examine the transformation of a retailer from a position of failure to one of success.

(Concern: Good Location But No Sales):

Once, I was traveling to Mumbai and happened to be in Breach Candy when I came across a showroom with an excellent location. Intrigued, I decided to enter the showroom and discovered a small department for toys. I spoke to the manager and was surprised to learn about the below-par sales of toys considering the shop's advantageous location.

(Main Problem: Not Getting As Many Sales As He Can Because He Is Brand Reluctant):

Upon studying the toy department, I noticed the absence of many potential toys from the shelves. I spoke to the manager about it, but he seemed reluctant to introduce new brands.

(Success: How He Become Zero To Hero After My Advice):

However, after engaging in a deep discussion with him, I managed to change his mindset, and eventually, he agreed to provide me with a sample order. What happened after that was unbelievable. The demand for the toys I supplied increased significantly, causing a disruption in the market. The situation became so intense that his competitors started calling me, either requesting me to stop supplying to him or asking for the same products, as all their customers had diverted towards that toy store.

The store also created a separate department specifically for my toys.

It was a moment I will never forget, and I was so happy to have played a role in someone's growth.

I have noticed that there are some common problems that toy shop owners face. Here are few of these problems:

1. Toy shop owners need to handle a huge number of items, somewhere between 10,000-15,000 different SKUs, as this industry offers a vast array of product options.

2. By and large, **toy shop owners are a one man army, handling** almost every function of the business themselves, including (purchase, sales, and operations). This leaves them stressed and burned out. Additionally, in many cases, the next generation is not willing to join their family business.

3. Training the right manpower is a consistent challenge for toy shop owners.

4. There is always a space crunch to display products due to the large number of SKUs.

5. Physical inventories often mismatched with records, resulting in discrepancies.

6. The inventory/sales ratio is very high, which increases the capital requirement to run the business.

7. Net profits usually reach their lowest point due to high competition in the market.

If you are a toy shop owner and are facing even one of the above-mentioned problems, then this instabook is for you.

Chapter 1

WHY I AM WRITING THIS BOOK!

Now, you might be wondering why I am sharing all these years of expertise and the hacks that I learned through pain and hard work for free.

Firstly, I am in love with the toy trade and it pains my heart when I see toy shop owners struggling to manage their business due to lack of knowledge.

Secondly, due to time and geographical constraints, I may not be able to personally meet each and every one of you to share my understanding and the knowledge I have gained over the years. This e-book serves as my small gift to toy retail owners and startups.

I hope these eight chapters will add significant value to your business and provide insights into its profitability.

"You can trust me as your reliable ride-on toy manufacturer and a "RETAIL MARKETING STRATEGIST."
~Harman Chhabra

Chapter 2

CONSIDER YOUR STORE A BRAND

*"Your brand is the single most important
investment you can make in your business."*
~Steve Forbes

Whether you are a first-generation entrepreneur or you have joined the legacy of your parents or grandparents, I understand that you deeply love your shop. Day and night, you are constantly thinking about how to take your business to the next level. Your shop holds immense significance as it has provided you with recognition, respect, and a livelihood for you and your team.

Did you know that your shop's name holds tremendous power? it becomes imprinted in the minds of your customers for years to come. Your customers perceive your shop as a trusted, convenient, and preferred place to fulfill the need for toys. They see, remember, and talk about it as a famous toy shop in their area. It's high time that you start viewing your toy shop as a brand and nurture it to become the most preferred toy shop in your area.

Let's understand the deep-rooted benefits of positioning your shop as a brand through a few examples:

Consider a modern-day retailer that has successfully positioned itself as a brand. They have designed their shop in such a way that customers have a superior experience when they come to buy the toys. When people visit this retailer and buy a toy, they don't feel the need to bargain; they simply make their selection of the toy and proceed to the billing counter. You may have encountered a similar situation when comparing a local kirana shop to a branded store like Reliance Fresh. While you might bargain at your local kirana shop, you seldom do so at branded grocery stores like Reliance Fresh or Spencers.

Your shop is a brand

If you don't create a brand, you will be treated as a commodity, just like any other product. And let me assure you, dealing with commoditization always poses a challenge. A brand, on the other hand, brings value and trust to both you and your customers.

Visualize and market your shop as a brand.

Chapter 3

WHAT IS YOUR USP?

*"Never follow the crowd otherwise
you 'll just be the crowd."*
~Bernard Baruch

How do your customers recognize you? Have you ever asked yourself this question? Every establishment and brand has its own strengths. It's important for you to find it out and develop your USP (unique selling proposition) around it. It's like finding and communicating your specialization to your customers. People love to buy from experts.

For example, if you have an eye problem, would you prefer to consult an eye specialist or a general physician? Most likely, you would choose an eye specialist! Similarly, your customers should know about your area of specialization.

You can ask these questions to yourself:

1. Are you a famous toy shop?

2. Are you renowned as a ride-on toy expert?

3. Is your shop known for providing a wonderful shopping experience with a wide range of innovative toy products?

4. Are you famous for offering the lowest price in town?

5. Are you known for your selection of newborn baby products?

6. Are you a renowned toy shop that offers a high variety of toys for all age groups?

Discover your strength, nurture it, and publicize it to leave a lasting impression in your customers minds.

Have you ever wondered how even a "Chhole Bhature" eatery, (a famous regional food in Punjab), can become the talk of the town and attract media attention?

You must remember to speak out loud about your specialization to create your unique selling proposition (USP) and stand out of the competition.

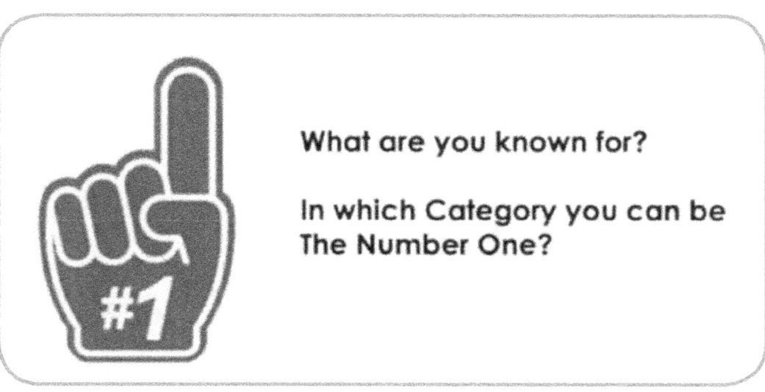

What are known for?

In which category can you be the number one?

In the case of our brand we sell a wide range of toys, but our primary reputation lies in being the experts of ride on toys. So, when I ask you to develop a USP for your brand, don't be confused. You can sell as many products as you can handle, but make sure to specialize in something and become well-known for it.

Think about the category in which you can excel and be number one.

Stand out! Create your own USP.

Chapter 4

MARKETING-YOUR BUSINESS GAME CHANGER

*"I do believe the modern
sales leader has to be a marketer"*
~Matt Gorniak

I understand that you have been working hard to establish your shop as a famous brand with a unique selling proposition (USP). From morning till evening, you are engrossed in operations and ensuring that your products align with your USP. However, in the midst of all these efforts, you often forget to actively invite your customers to your shop and showcase the best you have to offer them.

It's like you are doing your best to organize a wedding ceremony for your child, where all the decorations are in place and the best food has been prepared, but you forgot to invite the guests! In business, marketing is like inviting more and more customers to your shop, even beyond what you can currently handle.

A study has shown that an average entrepreneur spends 65% of their time on operations, 25% on products and only 10% on marketing. However, for the robust growth, it is recommended that an entrepreneur allocate 65% of their time to marketing, 25% to product-related activities, and only 10% to operations.

Where are you putting your energy?

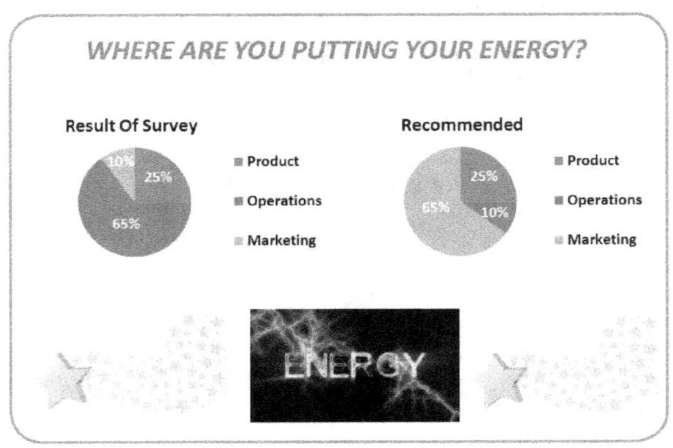

Most small businesses tend to neglect this crucial aspect of their operations. It's like having a Mercedes car with lots of accessories fitted, but with no engine. You end up exerting a great deal of effort to push it forward (doesn't it remind you of what you're doing in your business, pushing it throughout your life)? Marketing in business is like the engine in a car. You need to market your shop to create a pull that attracts more and more people to your business.

Let's consider the marketing strategy of a modern-day retailer:

- The retailer showcases kids and parents having a great time at their toy shop. The atmosphere is filled with vibrant colors, and their friendly employees demonstrating various toys to childrens. They proudly declare themselves as the finest toy makers in the world. They not only position themselves as a toy seller but also showcase their flagship shop as a tourist destination where kids and parents can have fun. This leads to a high footfall throughout the year and good business in terms of sales. Additionally, they organize toy hunts at their store, which attracts a lot of kids.

Marketing-Your Business' Game changer

Marketing is a game changer, remember this!!
Important: Don't confuse selling with marketing.

Selling is like serving a guest who has come to the marriage, and marketing is like inviting them to the marriage.

Chapter 5

YOUR MONEY IS IN YOUR HIDDEN LIST

Now that we understand the importance of marketing, you might be wondering how a small business can afford to do marketing? You may think that only big businesses can do it; they have a lot of money to spend on advertising on TV, radio, newspapers, hoardings, and other platforms.

Brother, today I will reveal a secret to you; how to market your shop without spending a penny and attract customers to line up at your shop, resulting in a revenue increase of more than 100%.

Are you interested in knowing this secret?

Many of us have been operating our shops for 5-10 years, and some of you may even be running ancestral shops that are 25-100 years old.

My question is: Have you ever created a list of people who have visited your shop and recorded their contact details?

The Majority of toy shop owners shake their heads in disagreement when I ask them because most of the shops engage in transactional business with customers and never bother to record their contact details in order to stay connected with them.

Don't you agree that if you invite your old customers to your toy shop, they would feel happy and privileged, and would be more likely to shop from you?

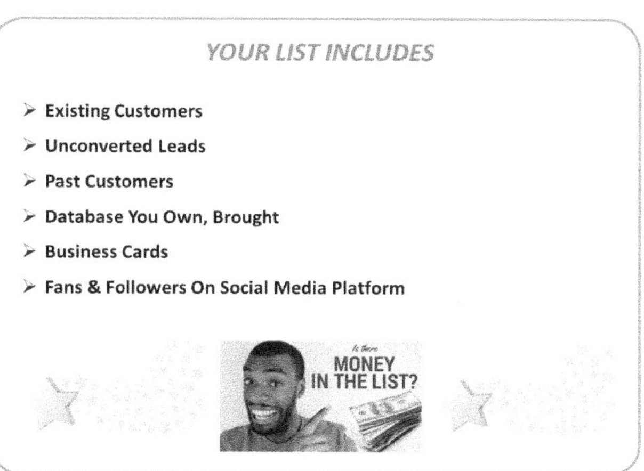

Your list includes:

- Existing customers

- Unconverted leads

- Past customers

- Database you own, or have acquired

- Business cards

- Fans & followers on social media platforms

Let me give you an example to show the power of having a list.

There was a small pizza shop in a town that was known for making very good pizzas. One day, a customer who had just enjoyed a pizza from that eatery asked the owner how he managed to attract customers to his shop. The eatery owner replied that he spends a significant amount on marketing through Facebook, radio, posters, billboards, and newspapers. The customer said, "Brother, what if I told you there's a way to increase your business without spending a penny, and it could bring you more customers than all the other channels combined? Would you be interested in knowing?" The pizza shop owner eagerly responded,"Yes, of course! Please bring it on."

"Today onwards, start creating a list of customers who order pizzas from your shop and record their contact details in your system, "the customer advised." After a month, start sending them special offers and information about new pizzas and dishes you offer. Keep a separate phone to record orders received through this list, apart from the other marketing channels you use," he added. With that advice, the person left, leaving the pizza shop owner intrigued and hopeful for the potential of this new strategy.

After a few months, the person visited the pizza shop again and asked the owner how his business was going? The owner was amazed with the results. He shared that he was receiving double the number of orders from the customer list compared to any other marketing channels, and as a result, he had stopped spending a significant amount on advertisements. The profitability of his business had increased fourfold.

I want to ask you: Why would you dig a well every day to get a glass of water when a well you have already dug can provide you with water for a lifetime?

Let's do some simple math:

- A study shows that Indian parents spend around ₹25,000 per year on purchasing toys for one child.

- Assuming the average lifetime value of toys for a child is (25000*12 years) =₹3,00,000 (3 lakh)

- The value of one name on the list would be ₹3,00,000 (3 lakh)

- The value of 100 names on the list would be 300000*100= ₹3,00,00,000 (3 crore).

- The value of 1000 names on the list would be 300000*1000= 30,00,00,000 (30 crores).

- The value of 10000 names on the list would be 300000*10000=300,00,00,000 (300 crores).

And so on...

After running a shop for so many years, how many people are in your list? The number of customers in your list determines the value of your business.

Nowadays, companies are valued on the basis of their active customer base. Start creating a customer list and invite your customers back to your shop.

Remember, the money is in the list! Activate it!

Chapter 6

JO DIKHTA HAI VO BIKTA HAI

Friends, you will surely agree with the old saying, "Jo dikhta hai vo bikta hai" (What is seen sells), and the same can be experienced from the fact that we end up shopping for more than what we initially intended from a store where products are displayed in a scientific manner. When toys are displayed appropriately, it increases the visibility and, consequently, the amount of products customers purchase. This encourages customers to visit your store more often to explore products that fulfill both their needs and unrealized desires. It disappoints me when I hear customers say that they feel confused while shopping for toys and, as a result, leave the store without buying a single toy. On one hand, retail shop owners handle a range of 10,000 to 15,000 products, but on the other hand, customers struggle to find toys that meet their needs when shopping in India. The usual reason behind this is that retailers tend to fill their shelves like a warehouse, thereby reducing the visibility of products and resulting in a poor shopping experience and low sales.

Merchandising and displaying the toys is both an art and a science. The right merchandise displayed at the right place, at the right time, in the right quantity, and at the right price can result in a great shopping experience and increase in sales.

5 Easy ways to increase sales with visual merchandising:

1) **Display age wise**

   Displaying toys according to the age group of a child increases the likelihood of customers purchasing more related products. For example, if you arrange all the toys meant for 0-12 month-old babies, such as brightly coloured toys, rattles, unbreakable mirrors, floor gyms, activity boards, stuffed toys, and small stuffed fabric balls, in one designated area, there is a higher chance that customers looking to buy toys for babies in that range will end up purchasing multiple toys instead of one or two. You must have noticed that when you buy a mobile phone from an e-commerce portal, it recommends related products like mobile covers and accessories. This tactic often leads to customers buying more items than initially planned.

2) Keep an eye on height

Displays that showcase items at eye level tend to attract more attention than the ones that force a customer to look down or up. The average eye level is approximately 61 inches, measured from the floor. To maximize visibility and increase sales, it's advisable to display new arrivals and more profitable items at eye level.

3) Hick's law -practice the rule of three

According to American psychologists William Edmund Hick, the time it takes for a person to make a decision is influenced by the number of choices available. Increasing the number of choices can lead to longer decision-making times.

Friends, it's a big myth that sales increases by keeping more options of a product serving a purpose. However, scientifically, having more than three choices for a specific purpose tends to confuse customers and reduces the likelihood of making a sale. Merchandising is an art that involves selecting the right SKUs (stock-keeping units) based on specific criteria to fulfill the diverse demands of customers while avoiding unnecessary duplication of items serving the same purpose.

4) Clear price point placement

Customers generally prefer not to ask for prices or spend time searching for them. Having clear price points displayed on products or displays enhance the shopping experience and makes customers feel more comfortable.

5) Bring in the excitement of new

Mark the new arrivals with pop-up signs to bring energy and excitement to the store.

Chapter 7

DIGITIZE YOUR BUSINESS

As a passionate entrepreneur, I am certain that you are always seeking different ways to make your customer's lives easier. After Covid-19 pandemic, the world has transitioned into a low-touch economy, and many of your customers now prefer having their needs delivered to their homes. The lack of digitization i n your business might be diverting them to other stores or platforms that offer the convenience of online shopping, digital payments, and home deliveries.

Over the last 10 years, with the boom of e-commerce, we have witnessed the delivery of almost everything, from clothes to electronics, right to our doorsteps. When a nearby restaurant can deliver cooked food to our homes, then toys should be no exception. The concept of an e-shop concept represents a new avatar of e-commerce. It helps you to take your store digital and reconnect with your customers digitally. The approach you take makes all the difference. E-commerce platforms like Amazon and Flipkart typically follow a transactional approach for business. As a result, the seller has hardly any relationship with the customer. However, the e-shop concept helps you to connect with your customers at a deeper level. In this model, both you and your customers know each other, fostering a sense of familiarity and trust. Customers can connect with you and make purchase with the same confidence as they would in your physical shop. There is a warmth of relationship and trust that enhances the shopping experience.

Furthermore, there are so many inexpensive tools available, WhatsApp, Facebook, and Instagram, to keep a connection with your customers.

It's high time you to start digitizing your business and acquire this new skill of connecting & selling online, to give your customers the convenience of shopping from their places.

Remember: Your customers are looking for you in the digital world, and you need to bridge this gap before someone else does.

Let me share an example of how a retailer near my home is increasing its sales through WhatsApp.

One day I was in a hurry to attend a birthday party and didn't have enough time to buy a gift. I remembered that I had previously visited a retail toy store near my home, and the manager had given me a WhatsApp number where I can connect and buy a toy without having to visit their store. I connected with the executive through WhatsApp, providing them with the age of the child for whom I needed the gift. The executive promptly shared a variety of toys options with me on WhatsApp, and I was able to choose and finalize a toy. The store efficiently delivered the toy to my home within a very short span of time.

Chapter 8

ADDING VALUE IS THE MAIN PURPOSE, NOT SELLING!

*"People buy people first
and then their product or services"*

Do you want your customers consistently choose to buy from you, even in the face of tough competition?

Are you noticing a steady decline in your profit margins due to the presence of both online and offline competitions?

If the answer of any of the above questions is "yes" then this chapter is exclusively written for you!

Have you ever wondered why we consistently visit the same family doctor every time we fall ill? Why do we prefer going to the same salon and having our haircuts done by the same barber? Why do we trust certain shops to buy gold from, even after all these years? There is a warm relationship and high trust in all the above examples. If you look deeper, you will find that you have developed trust and a relationship with them as they added value to your life over a period of time. By having a relevant communication over a period of time and giving super high value added information or advice which will provide immense benefit to your customers, helps to build a warm relationship and a buying environment.

When you consistently deliver massive value to your customers' lives, they not only develop a warm relationship with you but also place a high level of trust in you. You become the default choice in their subconscious minds. They see you as an expert and highly value your recommendations. Price becomes a secondary consideration for them because they strongly believe that they can obtain the best value from you, only.

Create a buying environment. People buy on emotions & then justify on intellect.

Chapter 9

MINDSET IS EVERYTHING

*"A million dollar advice
to regenerate your business"*

Brother,

You may have heard this phrase **"mindset is everything."** Today, I want to give you a million dollar advice. All the problems that you face in your business today is because of your old beliefs and a poor mindset. The results you are experiencing in your business are directly influenced by the actions you take in your daily routine. Unless you let go of your old beliefs and completely transform your current mindset, your results will not improve. Let me make you understand with an example.

One of my toy retailer in Goa who held the belief and mindset that expensive toys are challenging to sell in the market. As a result, he continuously operated in a **highly competitive market** and sold **cheap products** with minimum **profit margins.** He never made an effort to explore new customer segments or markets that had a demand for unique, high-quality products, where there was **less competition and higher profit margins.**

I helped him **change his mindset** by eradicating his **old beliefs and instilling** new ones. As a result, he began stocking and offering high-quality products, which led to him being acknowledged as **the No. 1 retailer of good quality products in his area.** His **sales and profit margins also increased** as he shifted his **mindset** towards the product and market.

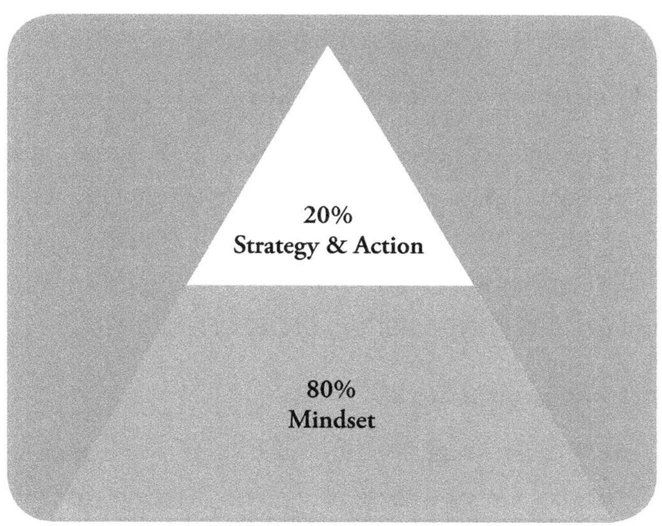

Chapter 10

LET'S RECAP

1) Consider your store a brand

If you fail to establish your store as a brand, it will be perceived as a mere commodity, just like any other product. This will inevitably result in challenges associated with commoditization. Building a brand brings value and trust to both you and your customers.

2) What is your usp?

Every establishment or brand has its own strengths. It is essential for you to identify and develop your Unique Selling Proposition (USP) around it. It's like finding and communicating your specialization to your customers. People love to buy from experts.

3) Marketing-your business' game changer

For robust growth, it is recommended for an entrepreneur to allocate 65% of their time in marketing, 25% to product development, and only 10% to operations.

4) Your money is in your hidden the list

Start creating a list and re-engage your customers with invitations to your shop. The money is in the list! Activate it!!!

5) Jo dikhta hai wo bikta hai

Merchandising and displaying the toys is both an art well a science. The right merchandise displayed at the right place, at the right time, in the right quantity, and at the right price can result in a great shopping experience and increase in sales.

6) Digitalize your business

It's high time you to start digitizing your business and acquire this new skill of connecting & selling online to give your customers the convenience of shopping from their places.

Remember: Your customers are looking for you in the digital world, and you need to bridge this gap before someone else does.

7) Adding value is the main purpose, not selling!

When you consistently deliver massive value to your customers' lives, they not only develop a warm relationship with you but also place a high level of trust in you. You become the default choice in their subconscious minds. They see you as an expert and highly value your recommendations. Price becomes a secondary consideration for them because they strongly believe that they can obtain the best value from you, only.

8) Mindset is Everything

Always remember the quality of your beliefs and mindset determine the quality of your actions and the results you achieve.

YOU HAVE 2 CHOICES

As you have reached the end of this chapter, I want to congratulate you on your perseverance and your willingness to make a change in your life and business. It demonstrates your level of commitment and your desire to make efforts for the success of your toys business. You are ready to take action and rebuild your business to make it more profitable and take it to the next level.

At this point, you have two choices. First, you can independently identify all the roadblocks within your system and work on resolving them. I have imparted knowledge to you and using this new understanding, you can do it yourself.

The second option is to have me by your side. I will conduct a comprehensive analysis of your system, identify the underlying problems, and guide you through the process of resolving them.

We can do this either in person over a cup of tea at my office or through a video call.

During our meeting, I will provide you with immediate solutions and help you create a plan to address any deep-rooted issues that may exist.

The choice is yours, and I am here to support you on your journey.

To book an appointment, express your interest by sending a WhatsApp message to 9911006165 or by e-mail at

harmanchhabra1987@gmail.com.

Looking forward to meet you.

With warm regards,

Harman Chhabra

Retail Marketing Expert